Like the Mountains of China

Like the Mountains of China

Edwina Pendarvis

Blair Mountain Press
2027 Oakview Road
Ashland, Kentucky 41101

Blair Mountain Press
2027 Oakview Road
Ashland, Kentucky 41101

Publisher's Cataloging-in-Publication

Pendarvis, Edwina D.
    Like the mountains of China / Edwina Pendarvis.
    p.cm.
    LCCN 2003105838
    ISBN 0-9666608-7-0

    1. Appalachian Region--Poetry. 2. China--Poetry.
3. Family--Poetry.   I. Title.

PS3616.E643L56 2003   811'.6
                                QBI33-1382

Acknowledgments

Some of the poems in this collection have been published previously. The author thanks the publishers below for including my work in their periodicals and anthologies. "August Afternoon" and "Sweetheart of the Air" *Wind Magazine*, No. 88, 2000; "Playing Cards" *Antietam Review*, Vol. 22, 2002; "Prodigal" and "Since I lived in Pikeville" *Pine Mountain Sand and Gravel*, Vol. 7, 1999; "To My Grown Son and Daughter Living in the North" *M Magazine*, Fall, 1997; "Augury" and "Prophecy" *Appalachian Heritage*, Vol. 30, No. 2, 2002; "Créche" *Gathering at the Forks*; "Visiting PCI" and "Augury" *Sow's Ear Poetry Review*, February, 2001; "Noon in Pedro, Ohio" *The Dickinsonian*, Spring, 2000; "In Old Xian" *Long Island Quarterly*; "Taking Prints" *Café Review*, Vol. 10, 1999; "Torso" *Grab-A-Nickel*; "Near Li-Shan Mountain" *Phoebe: Journal of Feminist Scholarship Theory and Aesthetics*; "Autumn Equinox," "Hall for Listening to Orioles," "Making Salt," and "Pastoral" *Red Crow*, June 2001; "Jenny Wiley's Return" *Journal of Kentucky Studies*, Vol. 16, 1999; "Farmer Brown Ascends the Gallows" *Caveat Lector*, Vol. 12, No. 1, 2000; "Floyd Collins" *Louisville Review*, Vol. 45, 1999; "Disparate Fates of Einstein's Brain and Osceola's Head" *Bones and Flesh*; "New Ghost" *Pine Mountain Sand & Gravel*; "Incantation On Darkness" *Tantra.* "The Illusion of Rivers" first appeared in *Now & Then*, Vol. 18, No. 1 (Spring 2001) © Center for Appalachian Studies and Services, 2001. Used with permission. "Meteor Shower" originally appeared in *Appalachian Journal*, Summer 2002 (Vol. 29, No. 4, p. 443). Copyright 2002 by *Appalachian Journal* and Appalachian State University. Used with permission.

Table of Contents

1

2

3

1

The mountains here look like the mountains of China.

Illusion of Rivers

My new pick-up truck
must be alluring.
Every now and then, a dragonfly
hovers above it, dipping and gliding,
lands lightly, uncertain as a shy first kiss,
flies away   then comes back,
in love too deep to resist.

Maybe it mistakes the truck for a river,
metallic-green
glinting in the summer sun.

Anyway, I *feel* like I'm steering a creek
when blue needles flirt
and flutter in front of me,
the tired Ohio flowing alongside,
solemn as the past already over
or the present constantly here.

My dragonflies must be the future—
darting just ahead on transparent, net-veined wings—
bright, no matter how brief,
no matter how faulty the premise.

Pastoral

The goat's out again.
Not Victoria, the Nubian,
or William Bonney.
Elizabeth's the one
who steals under the fence and into the pasture,
her alpine bloodline
way over-qualified
for this green
Kentucky hillside.
Slender-horned, she capers
up the gentle incline,
sure-footed and so certain
she'll find someone to follow
into the feed-shed full of hay for the horses—
sure destiny, smiling, will lift the lid
from the barrel of sweet-feed
and scoop out a handful
to hold under her
dainty, pointed
chin.

August Afternoon

Tony put on heavy work-gloves
so thorns wouldn't scratch his hands,
and we went four-wheeling, bouncing
up and down the trails on Cedar Creek.
Bullying our way, flattening saplings,
lumbering over fallen logs,
ducking low-hanging branches,
we tore through the forest, rode the ridges
and nosed down ravines.
Deep in the middle of a shady, green valley,
we spotted a doe, who stopped for a moment
to stare straight at us. A few yellow leaves
drifted slowly down.

Chinese Landscape Painting

You see him in the painting,
apparently insignificant,
a tiny figure far away, red-robed,
on the edge of a cliff
at the foot of a billowing waterfall.

The rain has stopped,
but its haze lingers above the river
and twines around Lung-hu Mountain.

Near the Shang-ch'ing Temple,
he stands, small
but vital,
a vermilion cachet
claiming nature's poem.

In jail,

a friend said,
prisoners make beer
from orange juice
fermented with bread.
Nasty tasting, he said,
but it gets you high.
Out of jail, he made a maple cane—
stripped the limb clean of bark,
soaked it in the creek for weeks,
then nailed it to a wooden bridge to pull it straight.
Cut into the wood by a grapevine
curling against the branch as it grew,
a slender groove spirals from its slender tip
to its graceful handle.

Some things are warped into beauty.

Playing Cards

My feet look pretty—
if I do say so myself—
white, with a dainty arch,
delicate, but strong . . .
a peachy pale tint.
They look nice against the blue
of my jeans. You can't tell
I didn't shave my legs this morning;
the stubble on my ankles
is barely visible, kind of nice, really,
when I brush my fingertips against it.
And the rug we're sitting on
is sage-colored, bluish-green
with darker bluish-green shadows in the nap.
Through the glass storm-door,
I see little new leaves blowing in the April wind.
On tv, some unhappy-looking people
are being interviewed about UFO sightings
and ghosts, but the sound is turned down.
Outside, one of the dogs barks
at a passing car.
I tuck one lovely foot under me
and lean forward to draw a card.

Prodigal

The oldest race lived without care
on acorns and wild fruit, on trees' dripping honey.
Death was, to them, only a sleep.
                    —Robert Graves

After a swim, gleefully stolen
from a muddy creek
on someone else's property,
we bumped along in our old truck
up and down the back roads of Carter County.
Warm July wind blew through the cab,
barely lifting our wet hair.
Dusty day lilies and wild carrot swayed
as we passed. A rustle
in the bushes to our left made us stop
to see what was disturbing the grove.
Through a circle of green leaves,
we saw a dun-colored goat
standing on his muscled hind-legs
in the midst of golden sunlight
and the circular drone of bees.
Oblivious to time and our idling engine,
the god Pan, hollow-horned,
stretched his long, pointed beard
toward the tender leaves
on a slender tree in an Appalachian thicket,
an ocean away from Arcadia,
centuries away from home.

Country Living

The sink's been stopped up for days;
the pipes are frozen,
but a strip of blue flame like a ribbon
brightens and warms the chilly air,
and Penny walks from the back
in a flannel shirt and loose jeans.
The smell of coffee brewing
fills the trailer's narrow rooms.
Outside, three muddy horses,
their manes dread-locked with burrs,
amble through the pasture; three goats
bleat from their makeshift sheds;
and two of the dogs tug a torn football between them;
heavy-metal music blares from the old, green Chevy
that passes by on the dusty road
a dozen times a day.

Sweetheart of the Air

My dad despised Amelia Earhart—
"that freckle-faced, gap-toothed runt."
Maybe his hate had nothing to do
with his being a pilot, too—
flying a little home-built plane
out of a grass airstrip
on a remote hilltop in West Virginia.
Maybe it had nothing to do
with his eighth-grade education,
with the mines closing,
with his stints selling dented cars
and scratched furniture,
with his rounded shoulders bending
his five-foot-seven frame
into an ever-deepening bow.
Maybe that five-foot-seven,
smiling daughter of the air—
who flew for the fun of it—
really shrank in his presence
to pint-size, the gap in her teeth widening
in proportion
to his ever-widening fear.

Climbing and Descending

Six thousand feet above the Ohio River and a whole lot
        else
I'm sitting in a painted tin tube alone with my son,
who's busy with dials and radio voices.
I watch the moving mountains of clouds
around us and remember
old warnings
against pride,
how it leads
to a fall.

I remember the fey, white maidens
who sold magic—when a mortal
reached for his purchase,
they grabbed his arm
and flung him
from the nearest cliff.

It's like Oedipus
in bed with his mother—
flying's something
you know you won't get away with.

I picture our plane—mortal-*cum*-spider—hanging
from a slender thread spun
by the goddess we've insulted.
Our propeller blades whir,
like somebody's scissors.

In the May Evening

I knock at their door.
Before they can answer,
a spirit-crane in the woods nearby
answers for them.
                              —Li Po

In her stone house on top of a hill tinged fuchsia
by redbuds, my aunt Juanita waits all by herself
for the end of cancer's long disquisition on her body.
She comes to the door in a pink, quilted robe, her
round head covered now with white down, her
brown eyes darker than ever before. She hardly
eats anymore, but her stomach is bloated. Years
ago, she let me play with her jewelry—costume
jewelry—all she had, except for her oldest necklace,
a gold basketball on a gold chain, a necklace Warren
gave her when they were still in school. Over and
over again, I dangled the golden ball above my
open hand and let it drop, its sudden heft always
a surprise, smooth and cool. The floor of her
three-room apartment shone like waxed amber all
around us as we played phonograph records
Warren sent from Korea—high-pitched women's
voices twirled brightly, like petals blown into the
room. Her black hair fell in loose waves to her
shoulders, and she wore a red silk robe, then,
embroidered with a wide-winged white crane
rising over mountains stitched small in blue thread,
to give the illusion of distance.

19

Appalachian Aubade

Not yet dawn,
but time for work. Out of the warm house,
down four icy steps,
and into the fog—a white tent
pitched from the street lamp.
I unlock the cold car.
Truck engines are already unwinding
down the dark highway nearby;
the watchman moon shines his tired beam
across frost-covered yards.
Trees along the road loom up as I drive—
a forest moves through the mist

until I pull into a SuperAmerica, its garish red and blue
muted by the sound of a fiddle from a roof-mounted
             speaker;

the tune cuts across gray dawn
like an elusive deer running through a high meadow
then gone.

Autumn Equinox

When I visited the farm last Sunday
to help my newly wed daughter perm her hair,
the autumn sky looked clear and deep:
perfect September weather. Even the dogs
were the perfect *dog*. Luke caught his treat in mid-air,
his big jaws snapping neatly just below my fingertips.
Shadow brought me a stick.

In the kitchen, Penny sat in their only chair,
and her young husband ate standing
while I parted her hair into tiny plots,
pulling each auburn strand taut,
rolling it—under and under—onto a curler,
clipping it snugly to her head.
We drank coffee till noon, then went outside.

Her long hair shaken loose
and shining, Penny cleaned stalls, and I picked beans.
Pale green pods and white pods speckled with red
hung in clusters like long-fingered hands.
Shadow and Luke barked at each other,
over who would fetch the clumps of weeds
I tossed into the air.

All afternoon, the sound of hammering
held us together as Tony built a bin for the tulip bulbs
          to winter in,
come the cold weather.
High in the wall of the toolshed nearby,
a fat copperhead—coiled between two planks—slept
under the eaves, like an idea.

Quickly

Today, one of the rabbits we've put on the dole
went into its trance—dark, oval eyes
unfocused but fixed
on distance.

A red-headed woodpecker
knocked, just under the eaves.

Tonight, the driveway looks white
in midsummer moonlight;
it curves downhill
past twin Lombardy poplars, crowded now
by untamed locust trees, tattered weeds,
and scraggly daisies.

The night air's prickled,
haphazard with fire-flies;
scattered stones light the way to the forest.

I know the oak is poised to open.

Winter Solstice

Three deer walked out of winter's night
and onto the mountain meadow—a stag, a doe,
a fawn, freckled silver by moonlight.

Maybe the mirror—
a deer-head mirror, cut from silvered glass,
pieces of glass for its face and ears,
glass for its wide, branching horns—maybe
the mirror called them.
Maybe the tree, unlit, in the corner
with ornaments darker than the room itself.
Or the midnight puff of the heater
with its answering row of little blue fires.
Maybe the young woman
standing barefoot at the window,
looking out of the dark room,
across the frost-covered yard
and past the cut-back rose bush,
past the gray shape of the truck,
along the gravel road, and up the hill,
where leafless trees, like antlers,
wait to carry the sun.

Springtime

Like a young colt running past a crack in the wall,
The light and darkness of almost a year have gone by.
                    —Ch'iu Chin

High above us a hawk circles slowly
around a jade-white sun.

A slide-whistle calls
though its years since anyone played it.

Last Fall, we buried J.O.
Now Spring shakes its wild, green mane,
bringing chartreuse light to the trees by the river,
where we meet again to remember.
Almost all of us are here—some above ground,
some under.

On the uphill path to the terraced graves,
Donald finds a black marble—a taw—
half-buried in the dirt, like a tiny opposite of the sun.

At the top of the hill, there's a preacher's stand of unpainted
            wood—
a floor and benches, a half-wall around three sides—
the opposite of a gazebo, it's a platform for watching eternity,
a sterner world than this racing, yellow-green morning.

Years ago, balanced on the half-wall,
forgetting the preacher,
the whistler's young sister, oldest now,
used to hook her arm around a tall pine
and, look out over the mountains. She could see,
before anyone else, the white smoke
of a long, black train approaching.

Since I Lived in Pikeville

they've moved the river,
dug a new channel
and dammed up the old.
The water must suffer amnesia,
knowing it's lost,
but not remembering where it's been.

Where we lived on High Street,
you walked off the porch right onto the road
or right into the living room, then
downstairs to the kitchen.
Propped up on stilts, our house seemed to lean
against the hillside. Below our bedroom floor,
the earth dropped away.
You'd think I'd have learned
to count on nothing,

but in dreams I row across the flooded schoolyard
and into the muddy theater
as though they weren't flickering
like a silent movie.
I hide behind the door of our tottering bedroom
and jump out at my sister again and again
as though we both still need lessons
in what not to trust.

Coronation

My daughter doesn't know it, but every birthday
she commemorates a fairy tale
with the red velvet cake she loves—
dark red with white icing—her grandmother bakes it
grudgingly—the icing won't stick to the cake—
lovingly anyway.

My girl never saw the royal coach moving slowly
through London's crowded streets,
the young woman inside, cloaked in ermine,
and soon to be crowned queen—
still queen now, half a Roman century later,
the empire shabby.

I didn't see it on color tv since the only color tv
I'd seen was a plastic sheet stuck to the screen—
a band of blue on top, red in the middle,
and, on the bottom, green.
Still, I remember it in color—
the real princess in a white gown
and a long, maroon velvet cape,
and—at last—on her short, curly, commoner's hair,
a jeweled and golden crown.

The queen mother's dead now,
and the young queen's an old woman, but
my mother bakes a coronation cake
for her granddaughter in the dead of every winter
for white snow, for blood red,
for the witch who blights every birth,
for all our pretty daydreams
and the uninvited truth.

To My Grown Son and Daughter Living in the North

Even in the South, the leaves have turned yellow.
Black snakes and copperheads coil underground.

Tonight I see you again as children
climbing the raintree—
clinging like bear cubs to its branches.
I dream the north wind brings you home.
You arrive all night,
like rain slanting through darkness.
Centuries ago and far away, on Turtle Mountain,
two children dreamed into being
played in the shade of a peach tree,
planted for the way it would measure the seasons,
while their father wrote to them from Nanking:

In southern China, mulberry leaves are still green.
Silkworms in Wu have now had three sleeps.

Hall for Listening to Orioles

Straw under the snow—
I don't know if you can picture
how wrong that looks—pale, yellowish stubble
poking through glistening white.

Mother wanted to put holly on her sister's grave,
so we drove to the cemetery,
its low hills strewn with tall pines
and hundreds of snow-capped headstones.
She waited in the car while my sister and I
looked for Juanita among the granite slabs
and the gaunt trees whipped by winter wind.
When we finally found her, under a mat of straw and
        snow,
we waved, and Mother stepped out of the warm car.
Each of us placed a branch of holly on the new grave,
making a loose bouquet of prickly leaves and glossy
        berries.

Standing in the bitter wind, I remembered my trip to
        China
and the Summer Palace near Beijing—
breezes blew politely from the lake
through an ornate, covered walkway
where an empress and her courtiers
once enjoyed the silken play of wind
against their skin. Their sleeves as soft
as birds' wings billowed as they strolled.
On the palace grounds still stands their favorite pagoda,
the Hall for Listening to Orioles.

Juanita's clothes, hanging in her closet, her yellow
        gloves
in a bureau drawer, still waft a faint perfume.
No one's spared the silent grave, but from the light and
        air around us,
Sister, Mother—no matter how wintry the weather—
from the scattered, sickly straw, from the whistle
of the wind, we can cobble, together, a summer hall.

Meteor Shower

Autumn, 2001

This night, the Leonids
are supposed to be brighter
and more active than they'll be
for the next ninety years.
My daughter and I get up at four,
pull coveralls on
over our pajamas,
and step out of the trailer
into the cold, dark yard.
Before we can throw our blanket
onto the hood of the car,
a star zips past, right above the shed.
We're out in the country
in eastern Kentucky.
Not far away—but in West Virginia,
Mother pulls the curtain aside
to watch stars crisscross the sky;
and on this same November night,
in a suburb in southern Ohio,
my son sits alone on his porch,
looking up and wondering
at the faint, blue-green trail
that chases each falling light.

2

Only heroes can save us this time.
—Ch'iu Chin

Torso

(from a photograph by Paul Strand)

A black and white photograph
of a woman's torso,
substantial as sculpture,
promising comfort
in the soft gravity of breasts,
threatening death in the shadow of flesh
that has been kneaded
and labored over
for years—

Here is Laocoön, Niobe, and Venus.
Here is Medusa, who could turn men to stone.

Crèche

January 17, 1991

Lit up like a Christmas tree,
the sky over Baghdad
sparkles with garlands.
Fire-spangled,
festooned,
the sky above
the ancient city glitters;
it twinkles, tinsel-strewn,
over mosques and minarets,
over hadji, mullah, and muezzin.
All night long, the dark-eyed children of Ishmael
attend a new nativity; they look to the west
and the gifts we bring.

Duplication

I hear a report on PBS
about an ivory-billed woodpecker,
and part of that report is a 1930's recording—
the toy-trumpet call and trochaic tap
of one of the last of these birds—
birds so exotic
they were called the "lord, god!" bird.
And I take it as another bad sign.

The old recording caught the call
and *tap*-tapping
so the bird's busyness
could be translated again and again
for us to hear at our nationwide leisure.

High-frequency images of these recorded sounds
flew through transcontinental air;
and this written report (dimly mimicking
glossy black and white feathers) on that broadcast
is even further removed from the lost inhabitant
of a last wilderness—

just the latest steps, I guess, boding an infinite
            regression
away from that one, long-ago woodpecker
who astonished with flamboyant flash
and comic, fantastical song
only live and in person, only whoever happened by.

34

Augury

On the side of the barn—
right in broad daylight—
a luna moth
flattens its phosphorescent self
against a gray oak plank.
It shines—stopping a summer day
in mid-flight—
so bright
it makes me recall
not-so-far-away coal towns,

where moths evolve into colors
closer and closer

to the color of soot.

Persistence of Memory

As if in a dream, the lion with a big mane slept
in tawny light slanting through the woods
where we played on the hill above the coal camp.
It lies in my memory like the long-ago copperhead
curled on a rock
by the creek where we splashed
and waded barefoot.

I'm still not sure
what's real,
and what's
not,

but I hear the dogwoods
are dying. Acid rain
weakens them
to the blight that circles
their trunks at the bottom.
They're fading
like children in a ring,
calling "ashes, ashes . . ."
and falling.

Some truths wait coiled
whether you're
ready or not.
Other truths depend,
like a watch from a chain:
tick-tock,
tick-
tock.

Drinks Before Dinner
Or, Let Them Eat Jewels

My friend, with her faith in money,
held out her hand
for us all to see—alexandrites.
Three tiny gems lay
like tumbled chessmen
pointing in different directions
on her plump palm.
The Romanovs are back, she said.
She'd seen one graciously nodding to guests
in a candle-lit restaurant
last winter in Moscow.
She said she cried at the site of the czar's assassination
and the gruesome murder
of his lovely daughters, spilling
blood and diamonds
from their little corsets.

An amethyst, too, big as an eyeball,
she held up between thumb and index finger
for us to admire. Shadows on snow
in an arctic summer seemed to shine within it;
but deeper inside, a flat plane appeared,
blocking our gaze from its violet center.
Nothing's as simple as it seems, I wanted to tell my friend.
*Purple light has the longest wave; try to see through to the
end.*

Summertime in the Ancient Capital

In Xian—now unprotected on the plain—
once a walled city thirty miles square,
people gather in the gathering dark
to watch television outside.
Ten or fifteen children and adults
sit or stand in front of each set;
red, blue, and green reflections flicker
and dance across their faces.
This is not far from the funeral vault
with all the warriors, not so far
from that ancient reign.

In Beijing

Some of the truck drivers
still hang pictures of Chairman Mao
from their rear view mirrors,
hoping his spirit might protect them
against accidents
and minor misfortunes;
but the West has arrived,
and at eight in the morning,
behind the New Century Hotel,
fifty couples in a roped-off arena
practice ballroom dancing to western tunes.
In an adjoining space
in the public square,
half-a-dozen old men and women
practice tai chi,
making their own artful silence.

Visiting PCI

So these are the bad guys,
blue tattoos twining around their pale arms,
embracing their bad mothers, their bad sweethearts,
their soon-to-be-bad children.

In this big room each little group sits,
leaning together on hard plastic chairs
under the gaze of a uniformed guard.

Families and friends talk and eat, play cards, and cry
between two paintings of wild animals:
a poorly drawn cougar on one wall,
a misproportioned elk on the other.

The room's lined with machines
the inmates can't touch.
They stand back and point
at what they want, coffee, chips, a burger.
Someone who loves them
deposits the coins.

In the back of the room, there's a dark, glass panel.
Behind it, three un-visited prisoners
wait for visiting hours to end,
so they can clean the empty room.

Calligraphy

Only by altering elements of reality to something vague and
unreal can you give the audience eternal resonance and open
up profound vision.

Tensho—
seal style,
reisho—
scribe's style,
kaisho—
block style,
sosho—
grass writing.

Scripts can vary from the flowing styles of Nasikh and
Thuluth to the angular Kufi.

European styles are myriad: the Insular Majuscule, or
Celtic, the Lombardi, Gothic

and graffiti . . . about stylez and crews, they rack cans
and hang out in tunnels, they get covered in paint, they
are the inner city, they are style Kingz, they have super
crazy perspectives, a value system based on drawing
ability and guts. Instant gratification as the sun rises,
and there's you for everyone to see. They're a side effect
of our culture, a hybrid of ART and CRIME

and all those pretty colors.

Numerology

MOMA's #5

A golden calf
doesn't need
legs.

Living
doesn't always
breathe.

Bold as ever,
from its dark red
background

the great figure—arabesque
chasing light—
leaps,

dances up the walls,
clanging,
bringing fire.

Unrap

It seemed innocent enough:
a grade-school talent show—a lip-sync contest.
The gym was crowded with parents
and grandparents, aunts and uncles.
Eighteen acts, ninety seconds each.
"Surf City," four boys with day-glo cardboard-
       surfboards
and four girls, sipping Cokes.
An eight-year-old Asian Michael Jackson in black
       fedora,
white tee-shirt, black jeans, and one white glove.
A little Alley-Oop with his baby dinosaur brother.
People clapped and craned their necks
or left their chairs and stood
against the wall for a better look
at their rouge-cheeked kids,
their nieces and nephews, their friends' children.
Then two black kids took the stage.
Their unrouged faces showed too much
of what rap is rapping about.
They were too real.
Their real presence in the middle
of the show—kids pretending to sing—
stopped the play.
Their rap was no rap,
dragging onto the stage
what no one wanted to see.
Like the twelfth fairy at the christening,
they forecast disaster.

With their schoolyard courage
and their schooled fear,
unrehearsed, in hooded sweats,
they went up against
the costumed, assenting kin
of all that doting crowd.
They hardly moved. They didn't act black;
their attitude was no attitude;
their lack of defense
offensive (*I could do that*, someone whispered)
on a night when the only black kids who won anything
danced in the background
for the young, white rappers
who seemed innocent enough.

Another Brief History

Imagine a plain in Pickaway County
and on it a compound of tan prison buildings,
where chain link fence and concertina wire—
intriguing spirals studded with barbs—
justify the margins. Two hundred years ago
what was left of the Peckuwe sept hated
this flat land, so exposed to the cold wind.
They missed old Picqua town, the one in the hills
to the south, the one with plenty of game,
the one with fertile land, the one on Mud River,
and, finally, the one Clark's soldiers pounded
with cannonballs, with lead pellets,
with iron-shod horses galloping
over campfires and crops,
one Roman August.

Now, this still-imperial August, near Upper Piqua
            town,
the one on the ugly plain, a tow-headed young inmate
sits outside with his mother
at a picnic table—among other picnic tables
and other men, women, children sitting—
and tells her he wishes he could see the hills from here.

Green Shore Weight-Loss Clinic

It's the biggest business in this little town—catering
to the health-conscious folk of eastern Kentucky.
In the plywood-paneled front room, all the chairs
hook arms, facing front, like shakers at a sermon
waiting for their cue. The less-disciplined molecules
of imitation-orange air freshener latched onto other
molecules in the air we breathe have already started
dancing, unbidden. It's spring outside, and dogwoods
are blooming, but it's February in here. Below the
calendar and a Norman Rockwell print, a typed
notice announces "we no longer treat people over
sixty." They still treat young women, though, who
wear faded shirts and black jeans and sit quietly
waiting their turn. They still treat young men. Two
walk in right now. The one with the grizzled beard
wears a camouflage ball cap; the other's flannel shirt
has a sweatshirt hood. Tall, and muscled from hard
labor, they sit down one chair apart from each other.
A couple of minutes later, the man with the beard
hands his buddy some dollar bills to pay for the
weight-check and the cursory exam. Everyone here
is part of a team. The nurses call out names at five-
minute intervals. The pharmacist next-door does the
same.

Cowboys

Thousands of kids of our time
posed for our separate photographs
astride a photographer's pony
and waited, the sun in our eyes,
for the shutter to snap.
Childhood of heroes.

We wore borrowed chaps and a cardboard gunbelt
with cap-pistols in white holsters
studded with red-paste diamonds.
A blue bandanna
you could pull up over your nose.

Even now, in this brand-new century,
after Vietnam and Watergate,
after sweat shops and maquiladoras,
after oil spills and slurries, after mountain-top removal,
after smart bombs and daisy-cutters,
now, even in the aftermath of fiery retaliation,
we still believe the impossible—that we can be outlaw
and sheriff

that the bad guy gets away
to hole up forever, south of the border

that good always triumphs—
bending down from his horse, lifting his gal to the
            saddle
and riding into the glorious, sun-bronzed future.

Noon in Pedro, Ohio

It must've taken days to paint—
a huge white dove shadowed with blue,
covering one whole wall of the kitchen.
On billowing, chalky clouds under the dove
stands a life-sized Jesus, white-robed,
clasping a man whose face we can't see
because he's turned toward the wall
and toward Jesus.

A beer in one hand,
a homemade tattoo on the other,
the artist tells us he lost his job,
misses his wife,
tells us he's going to make it though,
go to school, major in business
and graphic design.
Because I've got talent, he says,
I've got something.

As his little girl climbs into his lap,
he pulls her close to his skinny chest and keeps talking
about what he can do.

A few feet away, in the living room, his infant son,
bundled in a faded pink snowsuit,
sleeps on the couch,
the television blaring,
the emcee urging contestants on,
coaxing them to take a chance
and win big.

Hunting, Near Pedro

Not far from the bamboo grove on Johns Creek,
Tony brought his Ford Pinto to a sudden, lurching
            stop—a wild turkey,
a big one with a dangling, ten-inch beard, paced in the
            shade of a sycamore tree.
No gun in the car, drunk, and hung over, he and Tim
argued over who'd have to tackle it till finally Tony
jerked on the door handle and jumped out of the car
            and over a fence,
launching himself into the air, arms outstretched
to clutch the bird to him. The turkey squawked and
            struggled,
beating its big wings, kicking and gouging with its
            sharp spurs.
Tony hung on—wrestling in the mud and the weeds,
feathers sticking to his face and arms—all the time
yelling to his cousin for help.
Laughing at the desperate pair, Tim stumbled out of the
car and set his beer on the hood; he looked for an
            opening
and almost fell; reaching past the flailing claws,
he grabbed one leg, let go, grabbed the flapping wings
            and pressed them down, holding on
until Tony could get a grip on the bird's thick neck
and wrench it, hard.

In Old Xian

From the vermilion gates of the palace
came the smell of wine and meat.
In the roads were bones of men who froze to death.
                    —Tu Fu

In the forested hills east of the city,
are the famous hot springs, Tangshan,
where Ming Huang watered.
One mineral pool was made to look like a universe in
          miniature,
with an island in the center, of lapis lazuli.
On crisp days, a cloud
of fragrant steam hung over this pond,
and there Ming Huang and his concubines
amused themselves in boats of lacquered sandalwood.

Cloisonné

AD 713. Ming Huang's first New Year in power.
At the full moon, he had his people assemble a light-
      wheel
to celebrate their good fortune.
An immense wooden wheel
outside the walls of Xian—
50,000 tiny bowls hung on the wheel.
In each bowl danced a tongue of flame.
A thousand women with flowers woven through their
      hair
tended this wheel—which flickered against the night
like a galaxy come down to earth.

AD 1995. This is a strange meal.
Hundreds of small bowls assembled on long tables in a
      back room.
In each tiny bowl, a pool of color.
Women, their hair cut short, sit on benches
and paint flowers outlined by pieces of wire
they pick up with tweezers
and place carefully on vases,
bracelets,
pendants,
and rings
to be sold in the showroom
at prices they can't afford.

Mao Zedong's been dead for years,
but, for a time, women drank fire
alongside their brothers.
A time may come to rise again,
to paint their porcelain skin—

red phoenix bursting from a white throat.
A time may come
to rise against the new empire
with its painted smile,
its golden lips,
its ancient, ochre tongue.

Melee

The mood of a comic book
and all the diligence of a summer's day
crowded with whoops and cries
from the woods around us
a tattered dog, ticks on its ears

jimson weed pulls easily
from soft earth darkly remembering
an old barn burned down

giant zucchinis lie scattered
like green clubs dropped after a free-for-all,
both sides too fagged
to shoulder their weapons and carry them home

along the sunniest ragged edges
of the forest, thorny blackberry bushes—
green and red leaves, red and black
beads shining like a snake's eyes—
overpower the barbed-wire fence
and sprawl across the rusty bedsprings in the pasture

onto the highway and down the dirt path
we steal through weeds and bushes, through trees,
drop our towels on a rock and walk down
to the bank of the man-made lake—itself a medley

on the concrete bridge high above
where we're swimming
cars and trucks whiz by
out on the lake a blue jet ski zigzags after a red one
Penny points at an oil slick
and a dead fish in the water, close your mouth,
she says.

3

Seven or eight children have gathered to build a snow buddha. The buddha is higher than the children; and though it is only a pear-shaped mass that might be a gourd or might be a buddha, held together by its own moisture, the whole figure glitters and sparkles.

—Lu Hsun

Taking Prints

It's hard to fingerprint
the uncooperative dead,
their hands clenched in an unyielding
attitude. Stingy—
whatever they had been—
unforgiving,
forcing us
to sever stubborn hands
from useless wrists
or snip numb fingertips away
and press the stiffened squares of skin
between two squares of glass.

Funeral Vault of Qin Shi Huang Di

Orange fists raised,
splitting the air,
six thousand
terra cotta soldiers
wade out of the earth, fully armed . . .
no—they stand subdued:
six thousand soldiers
row after row
in empty-handed attendance—
dust-colored officers and men.

Twenty centuries underground.

Overhead, rain on poplar leaves.

In the vault, nothing sifted down
to the first Chinese emperor,
nothing
sifted down
to Qin Shi Huang Di—
whose comrades
stood guard in the dark—

whose comrades now
take up their watch
in the open vault
of the blue air

row after row

in the open vault
of the blue air
at Xian.

Near Li-Shan Mountain

On the Suicide of a T'ang Dynasty Concubine

This morning rings with bells from the east.
Already Yang Gui-Fei combs her long hair.
She rises
and walks through the mist—
on stone steps
her glistening feet are bare.
Hibiscus blossoms fall and float in her bath;
the wind's soft fingers lift her damp hair.
Above the pool looms Li-Shan Mountain,
a green, sleeping horse.

From her handmaid, she takes the white dress—
the emperor honors his most fair.
Through gathering tears, she sees
his crest: a golden eagle carrying a hare.
Soldiers, range, rattling their gear.
The weight of the knife
bends her slender wrist
as she kneels on a pillow
and prepares to make the first cut.
Night will drum from towers to the west.

Making Salt

It's been about three centuries now since Boone,
            skulking
his lonely way through iron-age Kentucke,
found mastodon bones lying around a salt lick
in the Cumberland Mountains.

Dazed, he looked again and again
at giant tusks jutting out of the ground,
at the huge yellow ribs of something like a pachyderm
with menacing pointed teeth.

There, in the heat of summer, the canny frontiersman
stumbled onto a plain of bones.
Inside the parched curve of their parentheses,
his sharp eyes spied the past—
a blue glacier pushing everything aside.
From where he camped amid brittle arches,
keen as he was, he couldn't see the gigantic wave
that would sweep soon from east to west,
washing away lives to found a continent on bones.

Squatting down by the fire, beside a behemoth,
he poured cold, salty water into a flat pot.

Jenny Wiley's Return

Easy. It was easy.
Orange and yellow leaves skittering across the clearing
whirled upward in an eddy of air.
After weeks of waiting, she simply put down the awl
and followed the colors into the forest.

Her moccasins made no sound,
or it was drowned in the groan of branches
creaking in the wind.
Axes of sunlight fell between the trees.
Leaves dangled and danced,
like her children's bright scalps
hanging from a war-shirt.

As she leapt from rock to rock across a sunlit creek,
an angry shout arose from the camp.
In her path lay a fallen log,
so she crawled deep inside,
face down in brown velvet.
Rain began to fall, drumming harder and harder
as voices like the rain came closer.

Finally the thunder rumbled in the distance.
In the quiet afternoon, a spider crawled over her cheek.
A gauntlet of stars arched above her.
At last she slept in the willow log.
When she awoke and climbed out, cobwebs clung to
          her face
and silvered her leather skirt.

She walked all day and into the night, almost into the
        river.
Listening for voices, she'd missed its whisper.
Traveling west with the water,
she went home,

where it was hard.
After years back home, safe with her husband,
years with new babies, it was hard each September,
not to put down her work and walk back to the forest,
looking for a creek to re-cross, a hollow log,
hard not to follow the wind
to the other side of yesterday
with its sky like blue meadows,
its innocent, clover stars.

Prophecy

Tenskwatawa—Tecumseh's brother—walks into the
      circle;
in his arms he carries a dead man wrapped in muslin.
When everyone is quiet, even the babies,
he kneels and gently places the body beside the fire,
then raises his arms to the shrouded moon.
From around his neck, he takes a string of beads—
pellets of flesh—and presses it into the outstretched
      hands
of the closest warrior. Tenskwatawa stops and looks
      all around.
With his good eye, he sees the friends who are
      gathered;
with his blind eye, he sees the friends he has lost.
As sparks dance skyward, Tenskwatawa—
"The Open Door"—speaks:
A nation is coming. Our people return.
Out of the shadows the buffalo leads them.
They ride like the hailstorm that darkens the sun.
Cast by the firelight, giant shadows snake through the
      crowd.
To the flickering beat of water drums, phantoms curve
across the lodges; the black feathers and horns of the
      dancers
are swallowed in darkness at the edge of the clearing.

Farmer Brown Ascends the Gallows

December 2, 1859, Charlestown, Virginia

One booted foot on the steps, he looks up
at the dangling noose and the blue sky.
Drums roll as he climbs; a breeze
touches his leathery cheek.
Beside him on the steps
and in the crowd of soldiers
wait solemn men in top hats.
Cannon surround the scaffold.
He stands at last on the platform
and looks again at the noose,
then through it to green hills in the distance:

"Beautiful," he says. "This is beautiful country.
I never noticed till now."

He'd kept his eyes on heaven
and the hell of this world and the next.
He loved the beauty of action.

The crops he raised
blossomed fire.

Self-Portrait with Gun

The little postman laughed first.
From the garden, crows burst like iron filings.
I laughed, bent double.
How would the chair defend itself?
That plastic, faux-something pattern.
Everybody in the pub was laughing.
Out in the hayfield,
orange and blue scintilla radiated
from the middle of his face,
his burning eyes,
his wheaten hat.

Floyd Collins

He fit the part of Loki, trickster,
living in a twilight world
of gravel, mud, and sweating rock—
long-nosed and skinny, at home underground.
No one could keep up with him, scaling walls,
straddling canyons, dropping into deep pits.
He'd been trapped before and gotten out.
Trickster, up and down, above ground and under,
in and out of the border world.
This time, he couldn't move; he was
wedged into the tunnel:
arms pinned to his sides,
one foot caught under a fallen rock,
a heavy limestone slab inches above his face.
His wool coat hung outside the hole he'd crawled into.
Shivering with cold, Floyd grew impatient with
            waiting.
When rescuers came, he asked for his pal Johnny
            Gerald,
who strung a lightbulb around his neck.
He asked for his brother Homer,
who stayed as long as he could,
holding a sandwich for Floyd to eat, tipping a cup to his
            lips,
touching his shoulder all night.
Neither best friend nor brother could free him.
When the tunnel collapsed, they couldn't even see him,
so he tried one last trick to keep them digging:

"I'm free, boys—come on down," he cried.

Homer lowered a quart of milk on a rope
and waited, calling to his brother:
"*Are* you free, Floyd?"

"Naw."

Against His Own People?

When the strike came,
trainloads of strikebreakers and guards
poured into Mingo County.

Company machine guns kept strikers away from the mines,
so they sniped from the hills.

After their camp was shot up by company thugs,
after Hatfield was killed, an army of miners—
some wearing their uniforms from World War I—
swore they'd march through Logan County
and on into Mingo to end martial law
and free their brothers.

When Mother Jones—who'd waded the creeks to sign
            them up
for the union—told them no, they couldn't win,
begged them to go home, even claimed
she had a message from the President
promising peace—
"Sellout," they muttered, "traitor."

Thousands of them fought Sheriff Chafin's men
in a guerrilla campaign through summer weeds and
            wildflowers
in the Battle of Blair Mountain—
the biggest battle since the Civil War—
till Harding sent in two-thousand infantrymen,
armed with mortars, and sent
the 87th Light Bombing Squadron,
a chemical warfare unit.

The miners gave up their weapons.

After it was all over, Mother Jones
begged the release of the men still in jail.

Harlan Miners Speak

"They called me a redneck."

"Is that a communist?"

"Yes."

"Do you feel insulted when they call you a redneck?"

"No, I don't care."

"What do miners eat?"

"Beans, cornbread made without milk, bulldog gravy—flour, water, a little grease. In summer a few pumpkins."

On the Long March

Luding Bridge, suspended high above the turbulent Tung
River, dates back to 1701. Nine chains covered with wooden
planks formed its floor; two chains formed each side.
                            —Edgar Snow

After walking six thousand miles in one year,
after crossing eighteen mountain ranges and twenty-
            four rivers,
thirty teenaged soldiers volunteered to cross the bridge
            at Tatu
to brave the Kuomintang, who had pulled up the
planks halfway across
and set up a machine gun on the other side.
Each barefoot youth carried a Mauser and grenades.

While the "little red devils" crossed, hand over hand,
hanging from the chains,
the Kuomintang set fire to the planks
and trained their gun on them.
Never looking down, the boys came on:
one fell, then a second,
and a third—eight
fell into the river below.
But the others climbed onto the burning planks,
and in the face of that relentless advance,
the enemy fled before
twenty-two youngsters,
black with soot,
clothes aflame.

The Disparate Fates of Einstein's Brain
and Osceola's Head

Both were put on display—
one in a jar in a research hospital,
one in a sideshow with Barnum & Bailey
after being used by a soldier daddy to scare his kids.
Guess which was where.
Einstein's brain, they weighed and dissected,
scalpeled and teased, pried apart pursuing the genius
          within.
Scientists sliced and cross-sectioned, cut away
until it looked like *hors d'oeuvres*, wrinkled, wedge-
          shaped *crudités*.
Osceola escaped at last after serving time as a freak—
a renegade fire crackled through his hair
and seared the parched remnants of skin,
burned him to a gray powder,
fine enough to be sifted,
light enough to be carried by the wind.

*Only You*logy

Nine years after he died, but live on video tape,
ex-wildlife poet, Allen Ginsberg, in cock-eyed
dedication to Walt Whitman and maybe too in
memory of Jack—his true friend who has pushed
his daisy so loyally up these thousands of days
since watering it long and hard under the Florida
sun—stands in front of a mike again and compares
himself to the classical river that's still never the
same river twice. Young once, he's sixty-two here
in 1988 at the Second Chance Café, trying to have
fun, singing without much of a voice, moving
without much rhythm, taking his first poems
lightly, "don't smoke" his main mantra tonight.
"Don't smoke, don't smoke, don't smoke, don't
smoke, don't smoke, don't smoke," the only words
he seems to believe enough to change into song
and into a river. Close behind him, at his steady-
gray-serge-tailored shoulder, beside his downcast
face, a quondam angel-headed hipster mocks the
hopeful vowels. From backstage, the voice of his
mother's ghost complains to her only son, "Is this
the wheel you have finally set to, this wheel
squeaking 'please, please, please' all the uphill way"?

Always a surprise

the peacock's feather fan lifts and opens—
sparkling, omni-eyed
even when it's veiled in morning fog.

Her hair a shining, blonde sheet,
Nicole's slender fingers
turn the key in the small box she pulls from a wall of
        small boxes.
She lifts the lid and slips another message inside:
If I die, he has killed me.

Murder is all "yes."

Caught in the ivory cage of needle teeth
or talons, rabbits look down,
away from death
and its flawless resolve.

Reassured by the ordinariness
of his familiar hand reaching for the Sunday paper,
turning the kitchen faucet, dialing an old friend,
she hopes for the best,
but writes notes to the future.

New Ghost

for Jim Wayne Miller

Barely breaking the flow of light,
you stand at the edge of the woods,
a shadow-man, finding it hard to leave the place,
the music, and the soft, dark night.
Hungry for words to speed your crossing,
you call on a friend.

Sleepless, the two of you
walk together, picking your way
across a rocky field, saying each other's poems by
        heart—
sowing salt
with hands like leaves.

Not until morning starts down the mountain
does your old friend stop and speak your name—
planing with sound a simple craft
to carry you through the narrow trace
and see you to your native ground.

Victory

When a man, black like himself,
tried to grab his Olympic gold medal,

young Cassius Clay, soon to be Mohammed,
already the greatest,
fought him off easily,

then walked to the river
and slung the medallion far away, into the muddy
water.

He never felt stronger, he said.

Incantation—On Darkness

Hush. No talking,
no talking. The snow is falling
and the wind seems to blow
backward.

In the house of twilight,
in the house of the clouds
the voice of thunder sounds once more.

Buried face-upward beneath the hills:
a copper-boned skeleton.
On his breast, a grooved ax.
Beside him a scraper with a perfect edge.
By his head, a clay pipe,
covered in mica—glimmering with rainbows.
Jars of ochre are placed around him.

He waits in the darkness.
Come, you who listen, his spirit restore.

Face upward in a pine casket
on the steepest slope
of the deepest gorge
lies a steel-boned workman,
his rough clothes in tatters,
no knife, gun, or ring.

Face down in the mountain,
a miner lies buried.
No powder-soft ochre,
no white pine protects him.
Nothing but shadow fills his eyes.

They wait in the darkness.

From the pond in the valley,
from the pool in the meadow—
from the whispering grasses—
the wind is rising.

Come, you who listen,
their voices restore.

From the silvery spruce
and the shimmering birch,
from the crimson maples,
the red evening I bring you.

No talking, no talking.
The snow is falling.

The wind
seems to be blowing
backward.

Epilogue

The bee tapping inside your car window
likes your worried look—and how you keep
glancing nervously at him
as you watch the road
for a place to pull over.

He's not so eager to get out
as he is pleased to make your acquaintance
and that of your car.
He's pointing out the physics
of the windshield, sunlight pouring through it.

And before long
you forget your object;
you're charmed by his nostalgic reminder
of the corporeality
of the invisible—by his coded essay

on the implausibility
of a transparent plane
as a means
of escape.

Notes

"Chinese Landscape Painting" describes a work by Fang Ts'ung-i, a Taoist who lived in the Shang-ch'ing temple on Lung-hu Mountain in the fourteenth century.

In "To My Grown Son and Daughter Living in the North" the two ending lines are slightly re-worded lines from Li Po's poem entitled "Letter to his Two Small Children Staying in Eastern Lu at Wen Yang Village Under Turtle Mountain." As translated by Arthur Cooper, the lines are "Here in Wu Land mulberry leaves are green,/silkworms in Wu have now had three sleeps."

In "Visiting PCI," PCI stands for Pickaway Correctional Institute, a prison between Chillicothe and Columbus, Ohio.

In "Near Li-Shan Mountain," I have taken liberties with the story of the beautiful, 8th century concubine, Yang Gui-Fei. Most stories say that the soldiers strangled Yang Gui-Fei as she and the emperor Ming Huang, with their entourage, tried to escape on horseback; but some stories say that she was allowed the dignity of killing herself. In either case, the incident did not take place at the hot springs near Li-Shan Mountain.

In "Prophecy," the lines in Tenskwatawa's chant are anachronistic; they are taken from chants for the ghost dance ceremonies, which were later in the 1800s.

Floyd Collins died in the cave sometime during the two-week effort to rescue him in a much-publicized incident near Cave City, Kentucky, in February, 1925.

"Harlan Miners Speak" is a found poem. The lines are taken from court transcripts in the book by Theodore Dreiser and the National Committee for the Defense of Political Prisoners, *Harlan Miners Speak: Report on Terrorism in the Kentucky Coal Fields.*

The historical details in "On the Long March," are taken from Edgar Snow's classic book, *Red Star over China*, about the communist revolution. The epigraph to the poem is almost a verbatim quote of Snow's description of the bridge.

The historical details in "Against His Own People?" are taken mostly from Elliott J. Gorn's recently published biography, *Mother Jones, The Most Dangerous Woman in America*.

The title of *"Only You*logy" refers to a 1955 hit song by The Platters.

Some lines in "Incantation—Ode to Darkness" are taken from translations of Navajo and Iroquois chants.